GERMANY
AND THE FIGHT FOR FREEDOM

THE GODKIN LECTURES AT
HARVARD UNIVERSITY
1950

GERMANY

AND THE FIGHT FOR FREEDOM

LUCIUS D. CLAY

GENERAL, UNITED STATES ARMY, RETIRED

HARVARD UNIVERSITY PRESS

CAMBRIDGE · MASSACHUSETTS

1950

EDWIN LAWRENCE GODKIN

1831–1902

Edwin Lawrence Godkin, editor of *The Nation* and the New York *Evening Post*, was born in Ireland of English stock, and took his degree at Queen's College, Belfast, in 1851. He published a *History of Hungary* and was associated with the London *Daily News* and the Belfast *Northern Whig* before coming to America in 1856. Here his letters to the *Daily News* on American public affairs attracted attention and prepared him for the task he assumed in 1865 as first editor of *The Nation*, to which he gave a scholarly quality, a breadth of view, and a moral tone that brought it recognition as one of the best weeklies in the English-speaking world. In 1881 *The Nation* became the weekly edition of the New York *Evening Post* of which Godkin was made editor in chief in 1883. From that time until his retirement in 1900 he exercised an influence on public opinion out of all proportion to the circulation of his paper. Editors throughout the country, whether in sympathy with his views or not, watched for his editorials on all important issues. He was exceptionally well read in economics, history and political theory, believed whole-heartedly in democracy, owed allegiance to no person or party, and was vigorous and fearless in expression. In 1903, by a gift to Harvard University, his friends established "The Godkin Lectures on the Essentials of Free Government and the Duties of the Citizen" in appreciation of his long and disinterested service to the country of his adoption and in the hope of stimulating that spirit of independent thought and devotion to the public service which characterized his career.

PREFACE

THIS BOOK IS DEVOTED TO OUR EFFORTS TO SECURE
a free Europe as a part of a stable and peaceful
world. When I was invited to deliver the Godkin
lectures last summer, I replied that I would be
willing to do so only if the invitation was repeated
this year as an indication that there was still a public interest in the German problem. The renewal
of the invitation showed that there was still an
active interest. This is most important, because
public interest is essential to a sound solution, and
the solution, sound or otherwise, is certain to influence substantially the outcome of the present and
continuing struggle for a free world.

L. D. C.

Biltmore, North Carolina
May 15, 1950

CONTENTS

1

THE STRUGGLE
FOR PEACE BY AGREEMENT   3

2

PROGRESS TOWARD   31
A WEST GERMAN GOVERNMENT

3

GERMAN POLICY AND   61
EUROPEAN POLICY INTEGRATED

GERMANY
AND THE FIGHT FOR FREEDOM

CHAPTER 1

THE STRUGGLE
FOR PEACE BY AGREEMENT

IN THE FIVE YEARS which have elapsed since the total defeat of Hitler and his minions, we have failed to find the stable peace which we expected would follow German surrender and which we sought to obtain over many months, in a number of international conferences, by agreement among the victorious powers. Today there still remains in central Europe the barrier line established in 1945 along the Elbe River in Germany as a boundary between military forces of occupation which was also to become the line of demarcation between East and West, between communism and democracy.

On one side of this barrier line, the ambitious leaders of totalitarian forces plot and plan to consolidate further the communist sphere of influence in eastern Europe and to extend it westward. On the other side, leaders of democratic governments, less coördinated in their several efforts but no less determined, take steps to prevent communist penetration across the line and concurrently to revive the love for freedom in those peoples to the east who have known and enjoyed its benefits in the past.

It was the creation of this line which placed between the former free countries of eastern and western Europe the communist-controlled eastern part of Germany. This resulted in a severance in communications which contributed to, if it did not make possible, communist domination of the political life in eastern Europe which led to its governments becoming satellite states. On the other hand, it was this line which stopped the threat of an unopposed onward movement of the Soviet armies and in doing so prevented fear from engulfing western Europe before its countries could reëstablish themselves and recover from the devastation of war.

The conflict of ideologies, sometimes called the "cold war," which rages now in equal intensity in Asia as well as in Europe, absorbs much of the

4

energies, talents for leadership, and resources of the majority of the peoples of the world. Man must devote his best thought to security, his sustenance to the maintenance of large fighting forces, and his inventive genius to the development of new and more terrible weapons of war.

Why has this come about? When may it end so that we may live in a stable world at peace with one another? These are simple questions which come to each of us. Unfortunately, the answers are neither simple nor easy to understand. Yet there must be a full understanding of why these questions are difficult to answer, of the world situation which brings this about, and of a foreign policy directed to finding these answers; for only in such an understanding will the way to solution be followed by our people and by the free people of the world.

From the day of final surrender, Germany has been a critical location in the conflict between East and West. Not only has it become the place of immediate contact in which on one side of an artificial line rest huge Soviet armies and on the other side substantial though lesser western armies, but also, within its borders, the struggle to win the

5

German people to one ideology or the other started immediately and has intensified through the years since victory into a continuing conflict of governmental processes, propaganda, and economic warfare. Hence, a basic starting point to an understanding of the full problem is to be found in an understanding of the German problem, of the differences which have developed within Germany and their effect on the problems common to Europe.

I do not offer to you special or expert knowledge on these problems, about which so much has been published, other than comes from the experience of four years as a senior United States representative in Germany. The conclusions derived from this experience have given me certain deep convictions. Since I can discuss the problems only in the light of these convictions, I claim neither to be dispassionate nor even wholly objective. However, if at times I appear critical of past decisions, I hope that my statements will not be so interpreted. It is easy in retrospect to find fault with the decisions of the past in the light of events which have followed. It is not criticism but prudence to analyze the record of events to prevent a repetition of the mistakes of the past in the future. It must be remembered that these early decisions were made in the atmosphere of the common effort to defeat an aggressor enemy and with the overwhelming desire, certainly of our people, to create a world in agreement in which differences would be resolved by reasonable men in conferences rather than by armed conflicts between nations. Of course, we may say now that the character of our opponent was well known and should have warned us that such a solution was impossible. In point of fact, we did not know it; and our willingness to undertake the experiment of international coöperation to demonstrate good faith in the effort to secure peace by agreement by our willingness to compromise our own views to reconcile them with the views of others accounts in large measure now for the high moral value of our world leadership and will be even more important as the history of the day is written.

President Roosevelt said, in January 1945, prior to the end of the war: "In our disillusionment after the last war we preferred international anarchy to international coöperation with nations which did not see and think exactly as we did. We gave up the hope of gradually achieving a better peace be-

cause we had not the courage to fulfill our responsibilities in an admittedly imperfect world. We
must not let that happen again, or we shall follow
the same tragic road again — the road to a third
world war."

We should continue to be proud of his brave
words and never for a moment be sorry that we
made this effort and that the present unhappy
world situation has come about through the intransigence of others than ourselves.

In order that the German problem may be ex-
plained in its proper relationship to the world
problem, the first of these lectures is devoted to the
struggle for peace by agreement waged so long and
so earnestly by the democratic countries who had
fought Hitler. With this background we will
understand better the reasons for the failure to
obtain peace by agreement and the consequent evo-
lution of American policy. We will then be able to
explore our present policy in Germany in relationship to European policy and what may lie ahead.

Our efforts to obtain peace by agreement were
started well before the surrender of Germany. Even
though our wartime alliance with Russia had never
brought about the frank exchange of information

and the full coördination of effort which marked our relationship with the United Kingdom, it resulted in a number of international conferences, two of which, Teheran and Yalta, were attended by the principal heads of government of the three participating countries. It was at these conferences that the broad principles were agreed with respect to the terms of surrender for Germany and for its occupation after surrender.

The first of these two conferences, Teheran, was primarily a war conference although the surrender and occupation of Germany were considered and discussed informally. These informal discussions accepted the division of Germany into three separate zones for occupation purposes, the transfer of certain territories to the Polish government, and the fixing of zonal boundary lines prior to surrender. After the Teheran conference, the three governments formed the European Advisory Commission in London to proceed from the informal discussions into the preparation of the detailed agreements which would govern the three powers in accepting German surrender and in the control of Germany. While the work of the European Advisory Commission had not been formally accepted,

9

its papers were available for the Yalta discussion and formed the basis for the German provisions of the Yalta Agreement. Thus it set the stage for the developments which were to take place. It is somewhat in fashion now to condemn Yalta. However, Secretary Byrnes has pointed out that our chief objective there was to secure agreement on the Dumbarton Oaks proposals for an international peace organization, thus making it possible to organize the United Nations before the difficulties of peacemaking intervened. This objective may well have colored our views on the German problem and made us more willing to accept compromises in the belief that there would be an effective higher organization to resolve the differences which were to be expected to arise in practical execution. Certainly, this was the prevailing view at the time that the Yalta Conference was completed. Public opinion in America felt that Yalta was a step forward to a better world. The *New York Herald Tribune* said that it had "produced another great proof of allied unity, strength, and power of decision." *Time* stated: "All doubts about the Big Three's ability to coöperate in peace as well as in war seem now to have been swept away."

10

In any event, Yalta had fixed the European boundary between East and West and had established three separate zones of occupation in Germany. It pledged the three occupying powers to a common policy which provided for the destruction of Nazism and militarism in Germany, the disarmament and disbandment of all military forces including the General Staff, the destruction of war equipment, the removal and control of industry, the punishment of war criminals, the exacting of reparations, and the transfer of compensating territory to Poland. However, in spite of these punitive provisions, it reaffirmed the principle enunciated in the Atlantic Charter that the allies did not propose to destroy Germany and that its people could hope for a decent life and a return to the family of nations when Nazi influence and leadership had been extirpated.

Three principles were embodied in the papers prepared in London by the European Advisory Commission, which now included France. Although these papers were approved by the participating powers in early May, there was no immediate move to place them in effect after surrender. The western armies were far in advance of the agreed boundary and there was considerable reluctance to their withdrawal. It is alleged that Mr. Churchill particularly opposed withdrawal until a stable Europe was assured. However, diplomatic exchanges between governments resulted in a meeting of the four commanders-in-chief in Berlin in early June, and their negotiations led to the withdrawal of the western armies and their simultaneous entry into Berlin on July 4, 1945. Meanwhile, the commanders-in-chief in their initial meeting signed and issued the paper prepared by the European Advisory Commission and designated as the Declaration Regarding Defeat of Germany. It announced the policies of the occupation and the assumption by the occupying powers of full responsibility for the government of Germany. Concurrently, a second paper was issued which established the Allied Control Council as the governing body for Germany but made clear that in the absence of unanimous agreement each zone commander retained supreme and sovereign authority in the zone which he commanded. Thus, the four occupying powers had eliminated the last vestige of national government in Germany and had replaced it with four commanders-in-chief. This was a fateful decision out of which has developed the present separation of Germany.

The first meeting of the Allied Control Council was held in Berlin on July 30, 1945, at the same time that the three heads of government were engaged in the Potsdam Conference. It is important to note that France, which was not a party at Yalta, had been accepted as a full and equal partner in the government of Germany and given a zone of occupation carved from the British and American zones. Nevertheless, even though the French representative was sitting in the Allied Control Council, France was not a party at the Potsdam Conference which was writing the rules which were to govern the actions of this Council.

In general, Potsdam reaffirmed and elaborated the principles agreed at Yalta. In this elaboration, the major points of agreement were the establishment of central German administrative agencies to have authority throughout Germany in specified fields under the supervision of the Allied Control Council; the pooling of the resources of all zones for common utilization; and the exacting of reparations through the removal of industry found to be in excess of that required to provide Germany with a standard of living equal to, but not greater than, that enjoyed by the other countries of Europe.

The Potsdam Agreement, sometimes called the Berlin Protocol, was to serve as the rule of law for the three signatory parties. It was never accepted by France, whose representatives always refused to accept and to recognize those provisions of the protocol unsatisfactory to their government. While, I am sure, our representatives leaving Potsdam had many misgivings, they felt as Secretary Byrnes has stated that "we had established a basis for maintaining our war-born unity." Moreover, agreement had been reached for future meetings of the Council of Foreign Ministers, which would include the French Foreign Minister, and it was felt that such differences as did arise under the Potsdam Protocol could be threshed out and solved in these conferences.

Certainly it was in this spirt of coöperation that General Eisenhower and I entered into the quadripartite government of Germany. During the remainder of 1945 it seemed as if this international experiment would succeed. Little difficulty was experienced in establishing the machinery for quadripartite government. There was an impressive record of legislative accomplishment in the early months. True, an analysis of this record would indicate that it was mainly negative: the enactment of measures to destroy Nazism and militarism and the putting into effect of punitive measures against those who had participated in the establishment of the Nazi regime. Little progress was made in constructive legislation, and all efforts to establish German central administrative agencies were defeated by French refusal to consider this question pending a final determination of German boundaries and the character of future German government. The principal discussion was directed toward establishing the level of industry deemed adequate to support the standard-of-living formula fixed by the Potsdam Protocol and determining the plants which would be removed from Germany as exceeding this standard. Even this controversial subject resulted in a compromise agreement, which, however, was never put into effect because the Soviet government refused to place the resources of east Germany in the common pool.

Meanwhile, the Council of Foreign Ministers held several meetings attempting to draft the terms of peace treaties which would be submitted to a peace conference. Recognizing the greater difficulties involved in effecting peace treaties with Austria and Germany, these conferences were devoted almost entirely to the drafting of peace terms for Italy, Hungary, Rumania, Bulgaria, and Finland. Although conferences were held in London in September 1945, in Moscow in December 1945, and in Paris in April 1946, little progress had resulted, and it seemed that Russia was in no hurry for these peace treaties to be agreed. However, in the Paris meeting of the Council in June 1946, sufficient progress was made for the Peace Conference to be convened in Paris on July 15. Even then, the recommendations developed by the conference were not considered so that the treaties could be formalized until the New York meeting of the Council of Foreign Ministers in December 1946. During the latter part of 1946, the difficulties in reaching agreement on these treaties had convinced our representatives that full agreement with the Soviet government might indeed be impossible to obtain and that we could not stand by with idle hands waiting for agreement with economic and political conditions in Europe favorable to Soviet expansion.

It is difficult to fix the exact date at which the Soviet intent to dominate Europe was evidenced. In the early months after the war there seemed to be a genuine desire for coöperation, and in Germany and elsewhere the representatives of the western countries met frequently with representatives of the Soviet government in an atmosphere of outward good will. This good will was directed particularly toward the United States. General Eisenhower was received in Moscow in August 1945 with a warm and, I still believe, genuine welcome. In Berlin, Soviet representatives insisted that the headquarters of four-power government be established in the American sector. Likewise, they had refused to consider anyone other than General Eisenhower as the first chairman of the Control Council. Senior Soviet representatives exchanged visits with our senior representatives frequently unaccompanied even by interpreters. This same relationship existed in Vienna and elsewhere. There was evidence of Russian suspicion of the other occupying powers, but not of the United States. Even the inevitable incidents which resulted from the close proximity of our troops were not permitted to interfere with these relations. It is

17

still difficult for me to believe that the Soviet government had at that time fixed its goal in Europe.

However, by the spring of 1946, friendly meetings and exchanges were becoming less frequent. The eagerness with which the Soviet government sought to execute those terms of the Potsdam Protocol which it deemed advantageous, such as the exacting of reparations, was offset by the adamant refusal of its representatives to accept the terms which they no longer deemed advantageous, such as the pooling of German resources. Moreover, the boundary line remained a rigid barrier which we could penetrate only for specific purposes with Russian escort. The unification of Germany which would have eliminated this line would have placed us in direct touch with the people of Poland and Czechoslovakia. It was becoming clear that the Soviet government did not intend to let this come about.

Also, the great allied armies had been demobilized and replaced with a small number of untrained troops, whereas the Soviet armies remained in their forward positions in impressive strength. In both the liberated and defeated countries, new governments had been formed promptly with their liberation or surrender. Logically, since Russia was an ally, these new governments contained strong communist elements. When the American and British armies withdrew from Czechoslovakia and east Germany, the surrendered and liberated countries of eastern Europe were separated physically from direct contact with the free countries, and western influence was reduced to the meager influence exerted by our representatives on Allied High Commissions. The Soviet armies continued in these countries in great strength and were not removed until pressure and intimidation had placed the communist elements of governments in strong, if not commanding, positions. By the spring of 1946 these communist elements were still not in complete control of the governments behind the iron curtain, but they were the dominating forces in all these governments. Thus, communist expansion had succeeded probably beyond the fondest dreams of the Kremlin. Still, there was no advantage to the Soviet government in completing peace treaties with these countries until its domination of their governments was complete. This accounts for the delaying actions of Soviet representatives in the international conferences which were continued throughout 1946. When the terms of the peace treaties were finally accepted, Moscow was certain of its complete control of the governments concerned in east Europe. It had failed only in Italy, which was still subject to western influence. It was ready elsewhere to destroy opposition parties.

Our representatives fully realized the Soviet tactics. They hoped that the response of the people of these countries to the peace treaties would result in free, or at least partially free, governments which would be receptive to western ideals. Nevertheless, they were determined that the conditions which had resulted in Soviet domination in eastern Europe would not be created in Austria or in Germany. From the beginning of the occupation we had remembered that our major objective in Germany was to bring about an elected, responsible government which, under adequate control, could be returned to the family of nations. We were sincere in our belief that only through this procedure could democracy grow in Germany.

At the April meeting of the Council of Foreign Ministers in Paris, Secretary Byrnes expressed his concern over the deterioration of relations between the occupying powers in Germany, and urged full consideration of the German issues which had brought this about. Mr. Molotov refused to consider the German question at this meeting, so it was carried over to the June conference. Here, Mr. Molotov on one day, in a statement designed to please French communists, attacked allied policy in Germany. On the next day, in a speech designed for German consumption, he urged an increase in the level of industry, called for plebiscites in former German states to determine their desire to break away from Germany, and pledged support in principle to the conclusion of an early peace treaty.

Our representatives were now convinced that the Soviet government did not desire to resolve German issues or to reach a German settlement, as economic conditions in Germany were deteriorating rapidly and were creating conditions favorable to communist growth. Moreover, we realized that the economic vacuum which existed in Germany was preventing recovery in western Europe. Unless there was an early revival of German production, there was little hope of substantial economic improvement in western Europe as a whole.

Secretary Byrnes thus determined it timely to

formally invite any or all of the participating powers to amalgamate their zones economically with
our zone and to coöperate in the economic management of the amalgamated zones to bring about
a more rapid industrial recovery. This invitation
was accepted immediately by the British government. While this action was taken in the interest
of European recovery and to prevent chaos in Germany which would have made it ripe for communist exploitation, we still hoped that our joint
action would develop some Soviet willingness to
compromise the issues which held us apart. Thus
we were most careful, in setting up the joint German Economic Administration for the two zones,
to limit its authority to economic matters and to
avoid giving it any semblance of political responsibility.

This important change in American policy was
announced by Secretary Byrnes in his Stuttgart
speech of September 6, 1946. Our American Secretary of State had gone to Germany to announce a
constructive policy, which we would follow alone
if necessary because we believed it in the interest
of all Europe. His speech, which was neither soft
nor mincing of words in defining German respon-

sibilities, pointed out that it was timely for the German people to have self-government and the opportunity to earn their living, and that "the American people want to help the German people to win their way back to an honorable place among the free and peace-loving nations of the world." While this speech did not seem to obtain the full recognition which it deserved in America, its importance was recognized throughout Europe. From then on, the European countries knew that the United States had expressed its determination to remain in Europe until stability came to alleviate the terror which resulted from Soviet intimidation. They knew in Europe what Secretary Byrnes meant when he said: "As long as an occupation force is required in Germany, the Army of the United States will be a part of that occupation force." Clearly this was a definite change in American policy. We still hoped that the United Nations organization would be effective; we still sought peace by agreement. However, we were no longer willing to let conditions develop which threatened freedom, and we pledged ourselves to stand fast in Europe and to work to bring about conditions favorable to freedom. We had taken the initial step in formulating a positive program for the support of freedom.

While the amalgamation of the British and American zones resulted in no miracle of economic recovery, the bringing together of the basic industries of the British zone and the assembly industries of the American zone assured steady progress. Moreover, this progress was placed under the direction of selected German leaders who now had the responsibility and the opportunity to improve the living conditions of their own countrymen. While it aroused immediate Soviet opposition which crystallized in propaganda charges in the Soviet-controlled press that we had taken the first steps toward the dismemberment of Germany, it was well received and accepted by the German people in the British and American zones. It did not result in a break-up of quadripartite government. This came about in part because the amalgamation did not result in German political responsibility. It came about even more because Soviet expansion had not yet been checked, and thus there was no reason for the Soviet government to disturb the existing relationship in Germany. However, henceforth in Germany, time was no longer on the communist side.

Although the New York meeting of the Council of Foreign Ministers again failed to consider the German problem because of Soviet refusal, it did agree to a meeting in Moscow in March 1947, which would be devoted principally to the Austrian and German issues. Prior to this meeting Secretary Byrnes resigned, and General Marshall took his place. In March, just prior to this meeting, President Truman decided that the Soviet threat against Turkey and Soviet support of a communist minority trying to overthrow the popularly elected government in Greece had to be met. These countries did not lie behind a protective screen of British and American troops as did the countries of western Europe. Still, they had refused to be intimidated and had earned the right to the support of other free countries. The United Kingdom which had been helping the Greek government, was no longer able to do so. Therefore, President Truman called upon the Congress to provide funds to extend economic and military aid to Turkey and to Greece. This was a far-reaching step. The Soviet government had rendered meaningless the provisions of the charter of the United Nations which pledged its members to "refrain from the threat or use of force against the territorial integrity or political independence of any state." Soviet veto in the Security Council made redress in the United Nations impossible. We had recognized this situation and had demonstrated our intent to help free and independent countries threatened by outside forces.

Secretary Marshall could have little hope that the Moscow Conference would resolve differences and thus improve relationships within Germany, which were then approaching the breaking point. By then, communist elements were in full control of the governments of the satellite states behind the iron curtain. If the opposition parties had not already been destroyed, the stage was set for the later actions which, when completed, resulted in the flight for life from Poland of Mikolajezyk; the removal of the Hungarian Prime Minister; the exile of King Michael; and the purge of Czechoslovakian government with the deaths of Masaryk and Beneš. Where the whip had not cracked, all was in readiness. In addition, communist parties, well financed and organized, were strong in France and in Italy. In March 1947 communist expansion was at high tide. Everywhere it seemed that the democratic forces were losing strength; initiative remained in the hands of the Kremlin. In this atmosphere there seemed little chance that the Soviet government would accept any terms in Moscow which did not guarantee its economic control of Germany and provide for a highly centralized government which would lend itself to communist exploitation.

Thus, no one was surprised when the Moscow Conference proved to be another forum for Soviet propaganda and invective, nor when it adjourned with no practical accomplishment. As General Marshall reported in a radio talk to the nation of April 28: "Agreement was made impossible at Moscow because in our view the Soviet Government insisted upon proposals which would have established in Germany a centralized government adapted to the seizure of absolute control." He might well have added that this insistence in Germany was only a part of the pattern which had been cut for Europe as a whole.

The Moscow Conference had brought the three western powers into a closer accord. France admitted for the first time that Soviet agreement was unlikely on any terms satisfactory to the west, and indicated a willingness to work with the United States and the United Kingdom to develop a common policy. Drew Middleton says in his book, *The Struggle for Germany*: "On April 11 [1947], Molotov four times rejected the pleas of French Foreign Minister Bidault that the Saar be integrated into the French economy. From that moment, the French Delegation moved closer in thought to the American and British Delegations and away from the Russians. The French people and subsequent French governments have not forgotten Soviet intransigence over the Saar. A number of American public figures have claimed credit for the fact that since 1947 French foreign policy on Germany has moved, slowly it is true, into alignment with that of the United States. This credit should go to Molotov."

While I agree with this observation, I think there was additional significance in this move. There had been no desire on the part of the free countries to develop a common policy against Russia. Soviet tactics slowly brought about a realization that the democracies must join together to maintain a world in which freedom could survive. The incidents which developed a common alignment of the western powers came about only from their recognition of Soviet intent.

In any event, it was clear to the western participants that the Moscow Conference had ended our high hopes for peace by agreement under the conditions then existing in Europe. Perhaps peace by agreement was impossible; certainly it was unlikely to come about, and meaningless if it did result, unless the conditions were created in Europe which would eliminate the two great fears which had made communist expansion plans successful — fear of want, the lack of economic opportunity for the individual to earn a reasonable living; and fear of invasion, the lack of security against aggression.

A lasting peace was still possible, but the challenge to the free countries was unmistakably clear. A stable Europe was essential to peace by agreement, and stability could be assured only if the free countries had regained their economic strength and their ability to defend their freedom.

Although the Moscow Conference had not resulted in a break, there is no question but that henceforth the western powers knew that stability must be obtained before agreement was reached or even desirable. This called for a drastic revision of our policy in Europe and for its coördination to the fullest extent possible with the policies of the free countries of Europe. Reluctantly we had to exchange our idealistic approach for a more realistic approach, even though it was an admission of the failure of the United Nations organization to achieve quickly the stature which we had hoped. Thus, the first phase of the struggle for peace had ended.

CHAPTER 2

PROGRESS TOWARD
A WEST GERMAN GOVERNMENT

THE EXACT DATE when the struggle of the free countries to obtain peace by agreement ended is difficult to place. Certainly at the end of the Moscow Conference in the spring of 1947 the free countries realized that agreement under existing conditions was impossible and that even if it had come about it would be meaningless. Communist expansion had then reached its peak. While the governments of the satellite countries had not been purged of non-commuist elements, the final purge could be staged at any time. Moreover, the possibility of communist victories in some of the countries in western Europe could not be overlooked.

Nevertheless, agreement had been reached in Moscow for another meeting of the Council of Foreign Ministers to be held in London in Decem-

31

ber 1947. Perhaps new conditions could be brought about in Europe which would make this meeting productive.

On his return from Moscow, Secretary Marshall stopped long enough in Berlin to direct a strengthening of the bizonal fusion to include the granting of some political responsibilities to the bizonal German administration. British representatives were receptive to this proposal, and we lost no time in improving and strengthening the German organization. Moreover, we determined now that the existing reparations program, based upon a unified Germany, would leave insufficient industrial resources in the bizonal area for it to become self-sustaining, and be established a new and higher level of industry. Thus we had laid the groundwork for the economic recovery of west Germany.

Secretary Marshall realized that German recovery, as important as it was in its struggle for Germany, would be of lasting value only as it was related to the recovery of Europe as a whole. The loss of German trade with western Europe was a serious deterrent to an improved economy. This was realized particularly in the Benelux countries where the idle Rhine ports and the lack of traffic

32

on the Rhine River were constant reminders of the part played by German production in a normal economy. Our real interest was to secure the return to a normal economy throughout western Europe.

Thus, in a speech delivered at Harvard in June 1947, Secretary Marshall offered the financial assistance of the United States to those European countries who were willing to coöperate with each other to obtain a common economic improvement. Foreign Minister Bevin of the United Kingdom was quick to grasp the import of this offer and immediately asked the countries of Europe who desired to participate in such a program to send their representatives to meet with him in Paris. Mr. Molotov attended this conference, perhaps in the hope of preventing its success. Whatever may have been his purpose in attending, he walked out of the conference. Although the satellite countries had indicated their desire to participate, the pressure of the Soviet government was more than they could stand and so, likewise, they walked out of the conference. The Soviet government proceeded in every way possible to attack our motives and to accuse us of a deliberate attempt to exploit the European economy. "Capitalistic imperialism!" was its cry.

33

In addition, Mr. Molotov announced the formation of a separate economic bloc composed of Russia and its satellites which had as its purpose the defeat of our efforts to revive Europe.

For the first time in the cold war we had postponed our efforts to create peace by agreement and had taken the initiative to restore in western Europe the conditions of economic opportunity under which the natural desire of man to be free would rise again to defeat the false promises of communism and totalitarianism. It is important to note that this major step in a new foreign policy was made possible by the presence of our troops in central Europe. Nowhere behind this screen was our offer refused. The immediate effect of our offer was apparent. There was a new hope in western Europe. Further communist purges behind the iron curtain did not diminish this hope, and subsequent elections in western Europe found communism on the decrease.

Our offer of financial assistance had included the bizonal area and the French zone. Thus, Germany shared in this new hope. Particularly its people and its leaders were elated at the implied association with other nations in a common cause.

34

Of course, time was required for Marshall aid to materialize. However, time was now on our side, and there was no further advantage to the Soviet government in delaying tactics. It was in Soviet interest to wage a war of nerves re-creating fear in Europe before the plan materialized. The program of the Cominform, made public in the fall, was clearly directed at the domination of Europe; but there were now two obstacles: in addition to the thin screen of British and American troops which could be penetrated only by war, there was the promise of financial aid to bring about a more normal economy, thus restoring the will to be free to the people of western Europe. Thus, the Soviet government determined a break in Germany to be desirable. Indeed such a break might force us out of Berlin and raise doubt as to our intent to hold our position in Europe.

This was not an atmosphere which promised success for the November 1947 meeting. In point of fact, at the last meeting of the Control Council in Berlin, prior to the London Conference, Marshal Sokolovsky seized the opportunity to attack the western allies in sharp invective which concluded with the charge that we were transforming Germany into a raw-material exporting country which would have to import its equipment from the United States. It is interesting that almost simultaneously with this tirade, Secretary Marshall had delivered a calm and measured speech in Chicago which brought out the divergencies of purpose concerning the future of Europe between us and Russia and expressed the belief that the restoration of Europe as a solvent and vigorous community would decide the issue. While his restrained, studied words still conveyed an invitation for Russian cooperation, they reaffirmed our determination not to delay our efforts to restore Europe because of further failures to reach agreement with Russia.

Ambassador Bedell Smith and I had been recalled to Washington in November to report our views on the existing situation. At that time, each of us independently reported that a break in Germany was inevitable and that it would be accompanied by an early attempt to blockade Berlin to drive us out. Thus, the outcome of the London session was forecast by preceding events. In its sessions it soon became evident that there was no desire on the part of the Soviet government to arrive at a solution, and that once again a meeting of the

Foreign Ministers was to be used as a forum for Soviet propaganda. Soviet charges culminated in the repetition by Mr. Molotov in almost identical words of the tirade which Sokolovsky had made in the Allied Control Council. Secretary Marshall in reply stated that these charges were designed for another audience and other purposes and that their introduction in the Council of Foreign Ministers made it difficult to maintain respect for the dignity of the Soviet government. The Council adjourned without even a time or place being suggested for another meeting. The Council of Foreign Ministers had broken up.

We did not witness this break-up with exhilaration, but rather with sadness over the failure of a "noble experiment." All of us realized that henceforth we were engaged in a competitive struggle which if it did not become a struggle of arms would continue as a struggle of economic resources, ideas, and ideals. We were engaged in a struggle in which we desired no territory, but were unwilling for others to acquire further territory or the control of additional peoples by oppression and the use of fear to kill their will to resist and false information to capture their minds.

37

In conferences following the adjournment of the Council of Foreign Ministers, Secretary Marshall and Foreign Minister Bevin instructed my British opposite and me to lose no time in granting a large measure of political responsibility to the Germans under our occupation. However, hardly had we received these instructions when Foreign Minister Bidault advised Secretary Marshall and Foreign Minister Bevin that the French government was prepared for the French zone of occupation to be joined with the British and American zones under an elected German government, provided that in developing the plans to this end concurrent consideration was given to the French proposals for security against a revived Germany, including particularly the control of the Ruhr and of those phases of German industry deemed to have war potential. Thus, for the first time, British, French, and American representatives were to meet in conference to prepare a common German policy.

We were most anxious for this planning to proceed rapidly, as it seemed unwise to create a political government in the bizonal area prior to reaching full accord with France. The preliminary conferences were held by the three western powers in London in February and March 1948. Representatives of the Benelux countries also attended these conferences. They resulted in substantial progress, which was reported in a communiqué at the close of the conference on March 5. The details were to be studied by the governments concerned prior to the reconvening of the delegates in April. The Soviet government recognized that this progress promised an early West German government. Hence, in the Control Council meeting of March 20, 1948, Sokolovsky insisted on consideration being given to the attack of the Prague Conference of the Foreign Ministers of Czechoslovakia, Yugoslavia, and Poland on the plans of the western powers in Germany. Obviously, this attack, which had been delivered to our governments, was not appropriate for discussion at the Control Council level. However, using the unwillingness of the western representatives to consider this protest as an excuse, Sokolovsky and the entire Soviet delegation rose as one and withdrew from the conference room. The Allied Control Council had ceased to exist.

The next step of the Soviet government to block further progress in west Germany, taken on March

31, was to stop the movement of passenger and freight trains carrying allied passengers and supplies across the border en route to Berlin. This was the so called "little blockade" of Berlin, and for a time it aroused great interest in the United States and abroad. Certainly it proved that our military policy had not been kept abreast of our foreign policy. In taking the initiative with the extension of the financial aid to Europe, there seemed little chance that war would result. Nevertheless, this could not be precluded as a possibility. Secretary Byrnes had recognized the necessity of a close coordination of foreign and military policy in October 1945 and had recommended the establishment of a Council of National Defense, composed of the Secretaries of State, War, and Navy, for this purpose. Later, this coördination was to be provided in the National Security Council. Undoubtedly, when we had embarked on our program of financial assistance to Europe, we realized that we had permitted the great military strength which we had developed in World War II to disappear almost entirely in 1947. Later in 1947 we embarked on a program of rearmament which, however, had made little progress in 1948. Thus we were not ready for war, and our responsible authorities were apprehensive that the Berlin situation might result in war. However, we had the moral strength to take a calculated risk in extending financial assistance, and I felt strongly that we must take it also in Berlin. I reported that evacuation in face of the Italian elections and the European situation was almost unthinkable; that the cause of freedom had lost Czechoslovakia, and Norway was even then being threatened. If we retreated from Berlin, western Germany would be next. Our position in Europe would be threatened. It seemed to me that if America did not understand this and did not know that the die was cast, then it never would, and communism would run rampant. Our government was willing to take this risk. Also, the British and French governments saw the danger, and the decision was made to remain in Berlin. Actually, remaining in Berlin under the "little blockade" was no real problem as the movement of allied personnel and supplies was easily handled with a very small airlift.

The "little blockade" had convinced us that it was only a question of time until the blockade was extended against the German civilian population.

41

Probably the Soviet government would wait to determine if it had been effective in stopping the plans for West German government. In spite of the blockade, the three western powers and representatives of the Benelux countries met again in London in April. Although their negotiations were long and involved, this meeting agreed to the amalgamation of the three western zones under a German government of real, if limited, power. Prior to the formation of this government, a constituent assembly would be convened to draft a democratic constitution for a governmental structure of federal type and of democratic principles which, when elected by the German people, would govern under an occupation statute which would specify the powers retained by the occupying governments. Agreement was also reached on the establishment of a Ruhr Authority, which would assure the distribution of Ruhr products in the best interests of western Europe as a whole, and of a Military Security Board, which would prevent German rearmament.

The reaching of this agreement made it possible for French military government to join British and American military governments in the currency reform of June 1948. Our efforts to improve the economy of the bizonal area had been handicapped by a lack of confidence in the existing currency, and its reform was essential to further recovery as was proved by the almost unbelievable increase in production which followed.

This currency reform provided the excuse for the Soviet attempt to blockade Berlin by land and water. The Soviet government believed that starvation of the civilian population would force the allies to leave Berlin, and it was willing to use this ruthless method to accomplish its objective.

It is obvious that currency reform was only an excuse because the "little blockade" had been imposed prior to currency reform, following the preliminary agreement reached by the western representatives for the creation of a West German government. The extension of this blockade to the civilian population of Berlin followed the detailed agreement which assured that this plan would be placed in effect. It was designed to re-create fear in Europe, which would render Marshall aid ineffective, and fear in Germany, which would stop the establishment of a democratic government in western Germany.

In a report to Washington at the time, I said: "The question now facing us was the most vital issue that had developed since Hitler placed his policy of aggression under way. In fact, the Soviet government has a greater strength under its immediate control than Hitler had to carry out his purpose. Under the circumstances which exist today, only we can assert world leadership, only we have the strength to halt this aggressive policy here and now. It might be too late the next time. I am sure that determined action will bring it to a halt now without war. It can be stopped only if we assume some risk." Our government decided that it must take that risk, and it found that the British and French governments recognized the wisdom of such a course. In the subsequent discussions within the United Nations and in the negotiations both at Moscow and in Berlin, it became clear that the purport of the blockade was to stop West German government.

To digress a moment, I think it important to understand the difficulties which are involved when three powers having a common objective are negotiating with a fourth power. Ambassador Douglas would discuss the important issues with British

44

and French representatives in London and then with Ambassador Smith in Berlin, me in Germany, and the State Department in Washington. British and French representatives were proceeding likewise. Any differences in viewpoint had to be resolved in London so that the representatives of the three powers in Moscow could proceed under common instructions. If differences resulted in negotiations among the three western powers in Moscow, they would have to be referred to London where the same process would be followed in their resolution. This was time-consuming and made the lot of our representatives dealing with the Soviet government, whose representatives were sure of their position, most difficult. Unfortunately, there seems to be no other way in which the independent free countries may develop a common policy.

As is well known, the immediate negotiations failed to resolve the issue, and Berlin remained under blockade. Fortunately, there remained enough of our air strength which we had developed in World War II to combine with British air strength in an airlift which kept two and a half million people supplied with the essentials of life. It must be remembered that the great success of the

45

airlift could not have been attained if the people which it supplied had not chosen the cause of freedom in the face of deprivation and suffering. Once again, unwittingly perhaps, the Soviet government had made possible the re-creation of the desire to be free within German hearts, which may indeed be the deciding factor in the struggle for Germany.

Meanwhile, progress was being made in West Germany in the drafting of the new constitution even though it was less rapid than we had expected.

Much had been done to condition the German people to a new political life. This phase of the occupation was overshadowed by the constant struggle between east and west, and yet perhaps more than any other phase it will determine the success of the occupation in the accomplishment of our objectives. From the early days after surrender, we had remembered in the American zone that the day would come when the German people would no longer be under occupation, and that the measure of our success would be the type and kind of government which would endure in Germany. Thus, in the fall of 1945, we had returned local government in the small towns and villages to German hands, and this move was followed

46

quickly by elections in the counties and in the large cities. We had also created four German states; and as quickly as these states could prepare democratic constitutions, we had placed them under elected German governments. Finally, we had created a Council of States to coördinate their activities and to give at least to the American zone experience in the operation of a federal government. The French zone had followed a somewhat similar pattern, except that it had not established a zonal organization and had retained all elements of zonal control in French military government. However, as the French desired a very weak confederated government for Germany as a whole, they had given substantial powers to the several states. While the British representatives had also returned local government to German hands and had created elected state governments, they had lived long and well under an unwritten constitution and therefore had little faith in written constitutions as such and hence made no effort to develop state constitutions. In point of fact, their inclination to a strongly centralized government had resulted in the states having less power than in the French and American zones. Zonal power was exercised by British mili-

47

tary government, although it called upon a German Advisory Council for recommendations on all important issues. Still, in all three zones political life had been reactivated long before responsible German leaders were to meet in a constituent assembly to draft a constitution for the new West German government.

In many other ways steps had been taken to encourage the growth of democratic institutions. It is impossible to discuss all of these steps in detail. However, some of them seem so important as to warrant mention here. The denazification program was designed to serve two purposes: first, to exclude all members of the Nazi Party and its affiliates from the early elections until the major Nazis could be determined and excluded from public life; and second, to determine these major Nazis under due process of law so that they could be excluded from participation in public life, thus making it possible for the larger numbers of minor Nazis to be restored to the full rights of citizenship.

In the field of justice, military government operated from the beginning under a rule of law. Germans could not be imprisoned without due process of law. The German laws were reformed to remove

48

special Nazi provisions, and the judicial system was revised to assure the prompt trial of those arrested for violation of the law. In our own military courts we extended the rights of habeas corpus to all who came under the jurisdiction. Always it was our purpose to show the importance which we attached to a rule of law. The German press was reëstablished as soon as carefully screened publishers and editors could be found, and this press was granted increasing freedom as the occupation progressed, including the right to criticize the occupation provided the criticism was not malicious. Unlike other western zones, we insisted on an independent rather than a political party press, which could come later when the independent press was firmly established. Experienced newsmen have stated that by and large the new German press is of higher order than the press of the Weimar Republic. Similarly, radio broadcasting stations were returned to German hands to be operated by semi-public corporations with their directing boards composed of representatives from all segments of society.

In the field of education, much attention was given to the writing of new textbooks free from Nazi dogma and to the reform of the educational

49

system so that even the poorest students would have the opportunity to finish high school and to undertake university training. Particular attention was given to the bringing of teachers and educators in every field from the democratic countries to confer and advise with German educators. Increasing numbers of German educators and students were given the opportunity to visit and study in the educational institutions of the democratic countries. It was our conviction then and now that our greatest contribution to a more democratic educational system in Germany would come about through such an exchange. "America Houses" were established in twenty-five German centers where American books, magazines, and periodicals were available for study. The success of these houses was attested when they received more than two and a half million visitors over a twelve-month period.

Labor unions were encouraged to re-form immediately after surrender. They became stalwart supporters of democratic procedures. Labor and management leaders were urged to meet with each other and to resolve issues by arbitration and collective bargaining.

These are but a few of the many steps which were

50

taken to develop an appreciation in Germany of the values of democracy and freedom. This does not mean that there were not many Germans who believed sincerely in democracy and who would form the nucleus for the development of a democratic government in Germany.

Perhaps even more effective than our efforts was the contrast between west Germany and east Germany. The west Germans were living next door to the totalitarian rule of communism and were receiving sufficient information across the border to keep them advised of the lot of their fellow countrymen under Soviet occupation. Indeed, the monthly movement of east Germans into west Germany, which averaged as much as 20,000, was convincing evidence of the hardships of life in a police state. A comparison of the political developments in east Germany and west Germany bears this out. The allies had agreed to permit the formation of democratic parties in Germany. The Soviet occupying authorities immediately after surrender interpreted this in their own way. Bringing in German communists who had spent the war years in Russia, they forced the old Social Democratic Party of the Weimar Republic to amalgamate with

51

the Communist Party to form the Socialist Unity Party under the leadership of the returned communists. Fortunately, the Socialist leaders in the west, who were proceeding to revive their party, were not deceived by this action; thus, the Socialist Unity Party was not permitted to exist in western Germany since it could not claim to represent the democratic socialists. There the Communist Party operated as such and not disguised in name.

In forming German state governments, Soviet military government started with coalition governments following the same pattern that was employed in the satellite states. However, in short order, real control passed into the hands of the communist elements. The leaders of other parties who were unwilling to become communist puppets were forced to flee to western Germany for safety. Soon even the real Social Democrats, accepted in the Socialist Unity Party, also withdrew from it to seek safety in the west.

Eventually, a puppet government was set up in east Germany composed entirely of German communists prepared to take their orders from Moscow. Of course the establishment of an East German government was intended as an appeal to all Germans, since as a puppet government it could be granted theoretically more responsibility than was given to the West German government. The German people were not deceived. During the blockade in Berlin they had seen the Soviet government expel the popularly elected city administration from the Russian sector of Berlin and replace it with a designated communist administration. In the suppression of the political leaders in east Germany, the concentration camps used by Hitler for similar purposes again became crowded. The press and radio of east Germany were fully controlled organs of Soviet policy and communist propaganda. Scientists, technicians, and skilled laborers were taken to Russia while their families remained in east Germany. It was obvious that the welfare of these families depended upon the productive output of those who had been removed to Russia. Able-bodied men and women were forced to accept employment in the uranium mines. The mass evacuation of industrial plants, which followed surrender and which greatly exceeded any removals contemplated in west Germany, was soon suspended as the Soviet government had found that it was more profitable to produce in Germany for export to

53

Russia than to continue the removal of plants. This ruthless exploitation of the east German economy had left want and misery. Moreover, a large number of prisoners of war, taken to Russia after surrender, were returned very slowly; and those who came back were in physical distress. While later an effort was made to restore the physical well-being of these prisoners prior to their return, the condition of those who were returned early was not forgotten, nor the unaccounted disappearance of a large proportion of these prisoners who had neither returned to Germany nor been admitted to be present in Russia.

The contrasts between east and west Germany were object lessons in the values of freedom. They made it possible to establish a democratic government in west Germany which was inaugurated with the sincere endorsement of the German people and the support of the western powers.

Thus, the conditions which existed in west Germany and their contrast with those in east Germany convinced us that it was timely for western Germany to assume the responsibility of self-government. We hoped for continuous and rapid progress in the constituent assembly.

54

As the work of the constituent assembly drew to a close in the spring of 1949, it seemed that the insistence of the French government upon a loosely confederated structure might still prevent West German government. This came in substantial measure because France was not satisfied with security measures. The discussions between German representatives and the military governors showed clearly that while there were no insurmountable difficulties in reconciling German constitutional views with the views of the British and American governments, there was little chance for their views to be reconciled with French views. I urged our government to call a governmental conference of the three powers to develop common understanding before the German constitution was submitted for formal approval.

Fortunately, our government had already arranged for the Foreign Ministers of the North Atlantic countries to meet in Washington in early 1949 to sign the North Atlantic Pact. The signing of this Pact, in which we solemnly agreed to join with the North Atlantic countries in a common defense against aggression, allayed remaining French fears and brought about an atmosphere which enabled the three Foreign Ministers to arrive quickly at a common German policy. The Military Governors were able to advise the Parliamentary Council that the new German government would be given liberty of action in administrative and legislative matters, except in a few reserved fields, and that military government would be replaced by a High Commission when the new government was formed. In urging prompt action by the Parliamentary Council, the Foreign Ministers stated specifically that their major objective was to "encourage and facilitate the closest integration on a mutually beneficial basis of the German people under a democratic federal state within the framework of a European association." This message was an inspiration to the Parliamentary Council to complete the new constitution. It was presented and approved in Frankfurt on May 12, 1949. The Parliamentary Council stated in the preamble "that it was conscious of its responsibility before God and mankind, filled with resolve to preserve its national and political unity and to serve world peace as an equal partner in a united Europe." With the formal approval of this constitution, West German government was assured.

56

Meanwhile in Berlin the Soviet blockade had continued throughout the winter. The Soviet government did not believe that an airlift could supply the city of Berlin through the winter months. However, this airlift, which had deposited only a little over 600 tons in Berlin on its first day, had developed into an efficient routine enterprise which averaged in excess of the minimum requirement of 4,000 tons a day even during the most severe weather and which placed more than 12,000 tons in Berlin on its peak day. Shortly after the Berlin blockade was imposed, a counter-blockade was placed in effect against east Germany. This counter-blockade cut off essential steel and other supplies from west Germany, and also reduced the trade between east Germany and western Europe. Economically the counter-blockade was more effective than the blockade. It could not be broken by airlift.

The Berlin blockade had failed in its purpose to intimidate the western powers and to stop progress toward western German government. It was no longer to Soviet advantage to continue it. As West German government approached reality, Soviet representatives to the United Nations entered into conversation with our representatives on the lifting of the blockade and counter-blockade. Again the abandonment of plans for western German government was suggested as a condition; but when this was rejected, the Soviet government agreed to lift the blockade provided there would follow shortly a meeting of the Council of Foreign Ministers. Interestingly and happily for me, the blockade was lifted on May 12, 1949, the same day on which the constitution for the new West German government was approved. The firm stand by our government and by the governments of France and Great Britain had nullified this last desperate risk of the Soviet government.

Shortly thereafter, in the early fall, elections were held in West Germany to the new Parliament, which then proceeded to form a government. The results of these elections were gratifying. As was expected, two strong parties emerged: the Christian Democratic Union and the Social Democratic Party. Neither of these parties had sufficient votes to form the government. However, the Christian Democratic Union united with other parties which shared its general views to form a coalition government, while the Social Democratic Party became the principal party of opposition. Both the Christian Democratic Union and the Social Democratic Party were parties of the center or of the left in the old Weimar Republic. The new coalition government was now the party of the right; this indicated the shift in basic sentiment which had taken place in Germany since Hitler had destroyed the old republic. Parties of the extreme left and of the extreme right showed negligible strength and, in fact, the vote of the Communist Party in the several states showed a decrease in strength over previous state elections. The new government was headed by men who even in the days of the Weimar Republic had advocated *rapprochement* with France and coöperation in Europe.

When the West German government assumed its responsibilities, we had ended the first phase of the occupation. The three western powers had moved far toward their major objective to bring about democratic self-government in Germany. However, political and economic recovery in Germany were never objectives in themselves but always had in purpose "to encourage and facilitate the closest integration on a mutually beneficial basis of the

59

German people within the framework of the European association."

The test of our German policy was still to come. Would the German people accept and respect a democratic federal structure and could this structure be brought within the framework of a European association? Obviously this required not only the establishment of such a framework but the willingness on the part of Germany's western neighbors, who had suffered so often in the past from German aggression, to receive the new government in their councils. Would the new German government work to bring about friendly relations with its free neighbors appreciating fully that only through such an association could there be assured a free and stable Europe? Henceforth, the primary task of the High Commission was to encourage the new German government to take steps which would win it the respect and friendship of its neighbors; that of the occupying powers was to urge the acceptance of Germany in the councils of western Europe progressively and as rapidly as it could gain respect and friendship. Our German policy was now fully integrated into our European policy.

60

CHAPTER 3

GERMAN POLICY AND
EUROPEAN POLICY INTEGRATED

WE HAVE SEEN how the sincere effort of the democracies to bring about peace by agreement failed. This failure led to the change in our policy which resulted in the Marshall Plan, the establishment of West German government, and the North Atlantic Pact. The attempts of the Soviet government to block progress in effecting the change culminated in the blockade of Berlin. They failed to accomplish their purpose. The blockade was lifted. West German government became a reality. The European Recovery Program moved ahead. Our German policy was now integrated with our European policy. It had received the approval of France and Great Britain.

Perhaps the integration of German and European policy deserves some elaboration. Our Euro-

61

pean policy may be summarized quite simply; although such a summary is certain to be oversimplified if we fail to remember that at all times our State Department must temper its over-all policy in the light of its special relations with the several countries of western Europe. This is particularly true of those European countries which have overseas possessions in the Far East. Nevertheless — summarizing our European policy as I understand it, at the risk of oversimplification — we are extending financial assistance to the free countries of Europe so that they may become self-sufficient and their people may have reasonable economic opportunity. We expect the countries which are receiving assistance to work together in the common interest and to eliminate trade barriers among themselves. We believe that economic recovery which restores the hope of livelihood also brings back the will to be free.

Concurrently we expect these countries to strengthen their own defenses so that they will be prepared to withstand sudden onslaught until we, acting under the pledge contained in the North Atlantic Pact, bring our great strength to bear against the aggressor. In order that these countries may progress rapidly we are not only extending military aid, but also, and at least until this aid becomes effective, maintaining our own armed forces in Europe. We believe that the risk of war becomes less as the free countries become strong.

We are also extending financial aid to West Germany because we believe that democracy can grow only where there is economic opportunity and because a productive Germany is essential to a sound European economy. We are continuing to support the democratic elements in German government. We have provided for security against a revived Germany through its disarmament, the control of potential war industry, and adequate arrangements for inspection. We expect these measures to allay the fears of western neighbors so that West Germany may be received among the free countries of Europe.

When we embarked on this program for Europe in 1947, we had not kept our military policy abreast of our foreign policy. We were willing to take a calculated risk because we could not wait to put this program under way until our defensive strength was increased. However, foreign and military policies were being coördinated in the National Security Council, and steps were taken without delay to rebuild our own military strength. Since we are a democracy without aggressive design, it is necessary for our military strength to be limited to that required for sound and immediate defense. This requires ground forces of sufficient strength to hold our most important overseas possessions and to protect our major air bases, with sufficient reserve force in the United States to reinforce the most vulnerable of our positions if war should come. This requires, too, an adequate Navy to maintain our lines of communication, as air power is not yet prepared to supply overseas positions. Such a naval force must be prepared to cope with the submarine problem.

Initially the roles of the naval and ground forces must be in defense. To gain time for the mobilization of our full strength, we must have a powerful Air Force of long-range bombers which in event of attack against the free countries can counter-attack at once at the heart of enemy country to destroy or to retard the enemy attack. There is much discussion now as to whether our military strength is sufficient for this purpose. These discussions are healthy and basic to our way of government. In such discussions our military leaders must always ask for more until our defense is invincible, recognizing that their goal may never be reached. They know that defense cannot be made so costly as to threaten a sound economic and social structure, but it is not their duty to determine the point at which such a threat occurs. It is their duty to advise the public factually of the strength of our national defense as compared with the strength it should have for invincibility. If the cost of invincibility is too great, the elected officials of government must determine the degree of risk which we are willing to take to maintain a sound economy. Certainly our military strength at present does not guarantee a quick and immediate defeat of aggressive attack. However, unless we are sure that it can prevent such an attack from overrunning friendly countries while we are mobilizing, it should not be considered as adequate nor abreast of our foreign policy.

In any event, our defensive ability in 1950 greatly exceeds that of 1947, and we are devoting far more money for its support than at any other time of peace. Perhaps some of our thinking as to the adequacy of our defense has come from our possession of the atom bomb and from our contemplated development of the so called H-bomb. Certainly these two new weapons of war increase our strength, even though their great threat is against civilian rather than military concentrations. While the power of these new weapons is recognized, military men cannot consider them to be other than new and more terrible weapons of war until proved otherwise.

Although there remains doubt as to the full adequacy of the measures we have taken, we have made substantial progress in developing and carrying out a military policy consistent with our foreign policy. The true test of its adequacy lies in whether or not it has enabled our State Department to take those actions deemed necessary to sound execution of our foreign policy. If we have refrained from positive steps to help the free countries because the calculated risk was too great, then our defense is inadequate. Only our Secretary of State can say.

Why has all this been done? It is our view that the countries which remain free need only to become strong to be able and willing to defend their own freedoms. When this comes about in Europe, the pressure of communism will be met and thrown back by the pressure of democracy. When it is obvious that aggressive forces can move only to be met by equally strong forces, then such a movement will never take place. When this comes about, the many people in eastern Europe who now live under communism because of fear will demand free elections, and with fear removed, one by one the satellite states will shake off their yokes of foreign domination and become free again.

A recovered and united western Europe has the resources with which to restore balance in Europe. An analysis of the strength of western Europe will show that its manpower, its industrial productivity, its management and technical skills more than suffice for balance. Certainly, West Germany with its industrious people and its industrial productivity belongs in this concept of western Europe.

Since our program was launched in 1947, there has been real progress in bringing the free countries of Europe together. These countries now form the Organization for European Economic Coöperation, and daily their representatives meet in Paris trying to solve common problems in the common interest. It is true that this organization has not yet succeeded in bringing about free trade among the participating countries by removing artificial trade barriers and obstacles; nor has it resolved currency exchange problems. It still operates under a payments agreement which has many defects. Nevertheless, during the life of the Marshall Plan there has been continuing and unbelievable economic improvements throughout western Europe. The production of today is substantially in excess of pre-war production. Both the European organization and our own administrator realize the inadequacies which remain, and are planning and working now to overcome them and to bring about if not an integrated, at least a truly coöperative and coördinated, western European economy.

At about the same time that the European Recovery Program was put under way, five European countries — France, Great Britain, and the Benelux countries — joined together in a western military union to place their military forces under a single Chief of Staff for a common defense. This was a major step forward in bringing the western European countries closer together, which was strengthened in early 1949 when these countries joined with us and other free countries of western Europe to sign the North Atlantic Pact. These countries are now receiving miltary aid from us and their planners are working with our planners to assure the best use of this equipment and to coördinate their plans for defense. This, too, is a major accomplishment toward an integration of the countries of western Europe.

Since these lectures were delivered, an even more promising step to Western European unity has resulted from the Schuman Offer to place the steel and coal resources of France and Germany in a common pool. This plan has been accepted in principle by the Benelux countries and by the West German government. It could not only bring France and Germany together but could also serve as the foundation for economic unity in Western Europe.

Moreover, the western European countries have formed the Council of Europe, and leading statesmen have pledged their devoted efforts to making this Council effective. It is true that it has no executive or legislative authority. However, it provides a public forum for the discussion of problems common to the several countries which will bring the light of public opinion upon their solution. It may well be the start to a Council of real and definite authority. Mr. Churchill has said that in this

69

Council "by our combined exertions we have in our power to restore the health and greatness of our ancient continent — Christendom as it used to be called. No longer a breeding ground for misery and hate, Europe shall arise out of her ruins and troubles, and, by uniting herself, carry the world a step nearer to the ultimate unity of all mankind." Mr. Spaak has said: "The machinery of a United Europe has been set up, but the most vital problems still remain to be solved. We cannot build Europe in a day. We must persevere in the course we have chosen until we have succeeded in establishing a United Europe upon unshakeable foundations."

Admittedly, this record of progress falls far short of an integrated Europe, but few of us three short years ago visualized this much progress. An integrated western Europe is no longer a dream. It has become the practical concept of realistic men.

There remain many obstacles to fulfillment. West Germany is not yet accepted fully in this concept. However, it is represented in its own right in the Organization for European Economic Coöperation, and it has been invited to send its representatives to the Council of Europe. Many fears are still expressed as to the way Germany will go. They come in part from some evidence of a revived extreme nationalism within West Germany. This evidence consists principally in the development of political parties of the extreme right and in the return to German government of former members of the Nazi Party. In an occupied country, divided against its will, there are certain to be unscrupulous politicians who will attack the occupying powers as an appeal to German patriotism. So far these politicians have been unable to attract large followings. They could be suppressed by the Allied High Commission, although such suppression would be a direct blow at freedom. In my own view, now is the time to be patient in determining the ability of the democratic elements in Germany to resist and defeat efforts to destroy democracy. They have been successful so far. Oppressive action against either the extreme left or the extreme right is in itself inconsistent with political freedom and the sound growth of democracy. The place to defeat extremists is at the ballot box. The return of Nazis to public office cannot be viewed with equanimity. On the other hand, we must realize that 25 per cent of the German population became identified with the Nazi Party or with its many affiliates. Recognizing fully that such a proportion of the population could not be excluded from the rights of citizenship without creating a cancerous growth on the body politic, denazification was directed toward finding and excluding from public life the major Nazis who were responsible for the growth of the Nazi regime. These men must be watched carefully and must not be permitted again to occupy positions of public power. But we must distinguish between them and the lesser Nazis who were restored to rights of citizenship.

Externally, there is still another problem — the full return of West Germany to the Councils of Western Europe. It is not difficult to understand and sympathize with the natural reluctance of the western European countries, who have suffered much and often at German hands, to receive West Germany on a basis of equality. However, it is not Germany who threatens world security today. Rebuffs from the free countries encourage the nationalist elements within Germany. These rebuffs are becoming less frequent, and the recent acceptance of West Germany in western economic councils and within the Council of Europe record substantial progress.

There are those who argue that a recovered Germany will look eastward rather than westward, particularly if the German people believe that they can become united more quickly with eastern support. That is a risk which we must take. It seems to me that it is not truly a great risk. The people of occupied Germany have seen first hand what totalitarianism and freedom offer. Russia has built a legacy of hatred in its exploitation of the east German economy, in its use of German labor for its own purposes, in the early excesses of the Red Army, in its treatment of German war prisoners, and in its oppressive conduct of east German affairs. While no people like to bear with occupation of their country, no corresponding legacy of hatred has resulted in the west where the occupying powers brought food to prevent starvation, extended financial assistance to bring about recovery, and restored political freedoms and the rights of the individual. There is, at minimum, respect in Germany for the standards of western occupation.

Recently some sincere Americans who have given much thought to the German problem and who have studied world affairs far longer than I have suggested the unification of Germany under an elected German government which would be allowed a police force adequate to prevent internal disorder. When this government was established, all occupying forces would be withdrawn and Germany, by agreement, would become a neutral state like Switzerland, a buffer between east and west to absorb some of the direct shocks between east and west. It is suggested that perhaps its security as a buffer state could be guaranteed by troops belonging to the United Nations. Such a concept requires faith in agreement, and certainly the record of past agreements with the Soviet government is not one to inspire faith. Moreover, the United Nations does not have security forces, nor has it been able to reach an agreement for the establishment of such forces. Even if there were such forces, it is difficult to conceive of their existence in sufficient strength to offset the great military establishment now supported by the Soviet government. If the agreement called for disarmament, there is nothing in the past which could lead us to believe that disarmament would follow. The buffer state would live under the shadow of the Red Army, and this shadow would be cast to create maximum fear with the inevitable result of communist cap-

74

ture of the new government. With our forces withdrawn from Germany, there would begin a new version of the cold war in Germany, a version in which we could not be successful. The new state, living in fear and unrest, would be a constant invitation to the repetition of the pattern of Soviet accomplishment throughout eastern Europe. Under the conditions which exist today it could not survive. Perhaps such a state could survive if the defense establishments of western Europe were built up to offer an immediate check to such use of Soviet strength. We may be sure that no agreement with the Soviet government with respect to Germany will be carried out unless it is disadvantageous and dangerous to the Soviet government to violate the agreement.

It has also been suggested that peace by agreement cannot be worked out between Moscow and Washington; that neither the Soviet government nor the United States heads a coalition which makes this possible and that peace must come about by agreement among all nations. I agree that peace cannot come about by agreement between Washington and Moscow. Certainly we head no coalition; we claim to speak for no one but ourselves.

75

However, we cannot ignore the Soviet bloc, which is more than a coalition and indeed stands forth against the rest of the world under the complete domination of its Russian masters. When we speak to Russia in terms of possible peace, we seek to consult with other free countries before speaking. In the face of the established Soviet bloc, we are attempting to bring the free countries into a co-ordinated defense of their freedoms. To do otherwise would be a return to isolationism. Certainly we would welcome return to a world in which all nations meet in equality and no nation is dominated by any other. Until such a world exists, we must be realistic.

Both of these versions arise perhaps from revived discussions for the ending of the cold war by agreement. This, too, is wishful thinking until we have developed within the free countries the strength which will insure that such an agreement will be carried out. Surely we have learned a lesson during the past five years and will never again bury our heads in the sands of paper agreements.

A major weakness in the execution of our policy to date comes from the failure of the free countries to use fully the past three years to rebuild their military strength. Our own military position has improved. Planning for coördinated defense is now under way in western Europe as our military equipment is beginning to reach the participating countries. Nevertheless, planning is still the order of the day, and the defensive ability of western Europe is not much greater than it was three years ago. If western Europe could find the way to a composite defense instead of individually maintaining armies, navies, and air forces, then defense of real strength could result quickly within present expenditures of funds. However, until this does come about, we must do our best to achieve real coördination of the strengths which exist and can be built up.

Some day, if Western Germany is to be fully received in the councils of western Europe, consideration must be given to the part which it is to play in the coördinated defense program. I am not advocating the immediate rearmament of West Germany; that is a decision which must be made by its neighbors, and even our support of this proposal could well destroy the progress toward an integrated western Europe. I do advocate the constant examination of this question by the statesmen of the free countries realistically and without prejudice. In the kind of Europe which exists today, Germany cannot be left undefended unless we expect it, dominated by fear, to fall under Soviet influence just as did the countries of eastern Europe. Therefore, the occupying powers continue to provide security for West Germany. This cannot continue forever. Germany cannot become fully associated with western Europe unless it contributes to the common defense. If a composite defense establishment could result, it might afford the opportunity for Germany to participate without raising again a fear of German aggression. No country contributing to such a composite force would have the over-all fighting strength which makes aggression possible. In recent discussions in Brussels, substantial although not full progress has been made toward the creation of such a force. Nevertheless, the question of German security, which relates so closely to the security of western Europe, remains a problem which the statesmen have yet to solve; it cannot be solved by running away from it.

The attention which it is receiving today is evidenced by a recent speech of Mr. Churchill in which he advocated West Germany's rearmament as a step toward increasing the defensive strength of western Europe, and by General de Gaulle who has recently suggested a federal union between France and Germany. To me it would seem more idealistic and realistic first to bring West Germany within the framework of Western Europe. With this accomplished, I believe that the problem would become relatively simple and easy to resolve.

I have not attempted to discuss our Asiatic policy, as my experience has been limited to Europe. However, as I understand it, we do not propose to shirk our responsibilities there either. In broad aspects, the Asiatic policy outlined a few months ago by Secretary Acheson follows our European policy. It may be more difficult to carry out for several reasons. We no longer have a foothold on the continent and must therefore hold island positions. Moreover, many of the countries remaining free in the Far East do not have long traditions of democratic government, nor stable economic structures. Hence, they are perhaps more vulnerable to communist penetration and exploitation. Moreover, because so many of their governments are new, they must be approached with sympathy and understanding.

79

If we look back on the record of the past five years during which we shook off the coma of isolationism and resolutely accepted the responsibilities of leadership which devolved upon our shoulders with victory, we need not be ashamed of what has been accomplished nor despair of what lies ahead. Our history as a nation is a short one, and our role of leadership is new. Time and time again, great countries have accepted the responsibilities of leadership, but it has always taken them years of experience to act with wisdom and success. We may expect to continue as a leader for years to come now that we have accepted the responsibility and have determined that the cause of freedom shall remain alive throughout the world, and that alien force will not be used to implant false ideologies on free peoples.

We are an impatient people, and we would like to accomplish our objectives quickly; but history does not move quickly. There has never been a period of world history in which aggression was not planned or used to carry out the mad ambition of those who lust for power.

In those few periods in which the world lived in peace for some years, there has always been some great nation which has maintained adequate strength to make aggression by others unprofitable. Great Britain, in the period in which it exerted its leadership to keep peace, did not relinquish its control of the seas because there was peace, but rather increased its control to maintain peace. Thus, in meeting the responsibilities of leadership which have come to us, we too must remain strong, conscious that our strength will not be used to wage war but to prevent it.

We must not be hasty in seeking agreement, because written words do not mean peace. If we remain strong and help the free countries of the world to become strong, and if it is clear that the combined strengths of all the free countries will be used to defeat aggression, there will no longer remain a possible profit from war, and peace will come about. Perhaps then even those mad with power will recognize the economic waste which comes from the maintenance of huge military establishments, and reduction in armament will follow. Perhaps then we can have a United Nations organization with security forces to assure peace. Perhaps then we shall find that the organization of the United Nations has not been in vain and that

81

differences among nations can be resolved in its conferences.

Surely thinking men everywhere must visualize the horror and destruction of a third World War. Surely, the men of the Kremlin would no longer wish to bring about such horror and destruction when it is evident that there can be no profitable return.

However, until balance is restored, there is little hope in peace by agreement. No matter how long it may require, we must remain committed to a foreign policy designed to bring about balance and stability. To do this we must be prepared to bear the heavy tax burden and to sacrifice as may be necessary in our expenditures at home to assist the free countries of the world who are less fortunate than we are, to the political, economic, and military strength to overcome any aggressor. Moreover, as we undertake this burden, we know that our sacrifices are not being made for aggrandizement in wealth, in territory, or in population, but only to preserve a world in which man may retain his dignity and in which man may be free to determine his own way of life. Only those who are willing and able to defend their freedom can be sure to preserve it. Unfortunately, in the troubled world of today, only the strong can be free. We must be strong to give of our strength to those who would be free but cannot be strong alone. To be strong in this purport is not inconsistent with our desire for peace. Thus, our foreign policy has as its intent the strengthening of free people everywhere in the interest of peace. This may not be a sure road to peace, but there is no surer way. In being strong, we must maintain in our strength and in our leadership the moral and spiritual values which, with fear eliminated, are the true goals of all peoples.